THE MONSTRANCE

Poems by
Bryan D. Dietrich

THE MONSTRANCE

Poems by

Bryan D. Dietrich

2nd Edition 2018
1st Edition Trade Paperback 2012
All Rights Reserved

Dark Recesses Press
657 Craigen Road
Newburgh, Ontario
Canada K0K 2S0

Edited by Jodi Lee
Cover Design by Jodi Lee © 2012
Cover & Interior Images by Bryan D. Dietrich © 2012
Author photo by Mary Werner © 2012

Library & Archives Canada ISBN:9781988837017
978-1-9888370-1-7

ALSO BY BRYAN D. DIETRICH

Praise for The Monstrance

"This book is a foundry of the fantastic. Bravo!"
—Michael Arnzen, author of *Proverbs for Monsters*

"With *The Monstrance*, Dietrich continues to emerge as one of the leading voices in contemporary dark poetry."
—Bruce Boston, author of *Dark Matters*

"*The Monstrance* is exquisitely framed to provide glimpses of life and death through the eyes of the Monster, his lover, his creator."
—Marge Simon, author of *Vectors: A Week in the Death of a Planet*

"*The Monstrance* is a fresh take not only on our favorite monsters that we love to love, but also on the strangeness of life as we experience it. Dietrich is a 'master mind.'"
—A. Van Jordan, author of *Quantum Lyrics*

"In Dietrich's hands, horror guides us to much more: a tale of thwarted family ties, a reflection on what's human, and a love story that accommodates forgiveness and transcendence."
—Ned Balbo, author of *The Trials of Edgar Poe and Other Poems*

Acknowledgments

I would like to thank the following journals in which some of these poems have appeared:

American Literary Review:
"On the Anastasis of Monsters"

Dissections:
"The Monster Attends Mass"
"The Monster the Master and the Windmill"
"The Monster's Retirement"
"The Monster's Last Lesson"
"Creature Comforts"

The Distillery:
"Belgrade"
"Florence"
"Transylvania"

The Dominion Review:
"Venice"
"Constantinople"
"Jan. 21, 1870"
"Apr. 13, 1870"
"Sep. 1, 1871"

The Laurel Review:
"The Monster and the Gypsy"
"The Monster Nodding"

Mars Hill Review:
"Frankenstein"
"Dec. 30, 1870"
"Oct. 7, 1871"
"On Absalom"

Northwest Review:
"On Reasons for Going to Hell"

Roswell Literary Review:
"The Monster's Brain"
"The Monster's First Lesson"
"The Monster Among the Nightingales"
"The Monster Learns About Fire, Again"
"The Monster and the Gypsy Join the Circus"

Strange Horizons:
"The Monster Learns to Read"

Naked City:
"The Monster and the Little Miss"
"The Monster Considers Progeny"

The following poems also appeared in *Universal Monsters*, published by Word Press; they reappear here by permission:

"The Monster and the Gypsy"
"The Monster Nodding"
"Constantinople"
"Venice"
"The Monster Attends Mass"

Finally, I would like to thank Alice Stewart, Scott Cairns, Bruce Bond, Giles Mitchell, Scott Simpkins, Cynthia Macdonald, Andrew Hudgins, Richard Howard, William Trowbridge, Shawn Sturgeon, Grant Sisk, Tim Richardson, Vicky Santiesteban, Sean Landry, Yula Flournoy, Bob and Carmen, Meg and Clint, John and Becky, Curtis Shumaker, Ze Bernardinello, Mary Werner, Rich Ristow, Jodi Lee, Mike Arnzen, Bruce Boston, Marge Simon, A. Van Jordan, Ned Balbo, and Gina and Nick for helping to keep the kites flying and the pitchforks at bay.

Dedication

For my sisters.
You gave me monsters.

Monstrance /ˈmän-strəns/ n.
An open or transparent receptacle for the exposition of the consecrated Host, or (occasionally) for the bones of saints.

Table of Contents

THE MASTER DIARIES

THE MONSTER: Part II

EPILOGUE

Afterword

INTRODUCTION TO THE MONSTRANCE
Michael A. Arnzen

It is so tempting to say that, as a poet, Bryan D. Dietrich is just like Dr. Frankenstein himself: *a mad creator, a creative master, a Promethean player with soulfire….*

And he sure as hell is.

But his poems are more than just the creations of his mad genius. They are *re*-creations. Adaptations. Playful revisions of texts that already exist in the popular imagination, lending them a depth that most people wouldn't recognize without his poetry to show them. The critic Veronica Hollinger once wrote that Bryan's work illuminates the "mythic power in even our most B-grade popular fantasies," a power we tap into when we play out our lives in "the guise of our fictional avatars." This is true of the great bulk of the wonderful work he's created in his lifetime—from warping the worlds of superheroes like *Wonder Woman* to mashing up the monsters from classic horror movies to reworking weird tales into poems that are even…weirder. Bryan constantly draws inspiration from superhero comics and monster films and pulp fictions and his lifelong journey through these texts—these memories—have sustained a remarkable career in poetry that shows us what makes their myths so potent and painful and powerful.

This is particularly evident in a book of his from 2007 that I simply adore, called *Universal Monsters*. I suspect Bryan wrote it for fun, but it is seriously good poetry. And by seriously good I don't just mean literary—I mean transformative. Genre-changing. I heard him read from this book at a conference we both have been attending together for almost two decades now (the International Conference of the Fantastic in the Arts) and the excerpts he shared simply floored me. *This,* I thought, *is what a Master Genre Poet sounds like.*

I have won awards for my writing, and I have spent hours

and hours crafting one single line, but Bryan's work made me feel like a total pretender…or at least very lazy, by comparison. Never had I heard a poet deliver *formal lyrical verse* in a way that wasn't dry or boring but downright lively. But beyond that, it was so profoundly well-wrought—it was almost as if Mary Shelley herself (or maybe her husband) had come back from the dead to reclaim the creature she had created that had been cast in film. It was clever and witty and complex. It was…smart…but not snobby. I think I may have even gushed in praise over cocktails that night and addressed him to his face as "Master"…I can't remember.

All I know is that he later was generous enough to share a print copy of the full book with me shortly before it came out, and I gushed all over again—and if I was tipsy that second time I gushed, it was entirely due to the intoxicating nature of his lyrical writing. I gushed in print, penning a review that he would later include as a "blurb" on the back of that book, one that Bryan tells me is one of his favorites of all time. I still mean it and I bring it up now because I feel much the same way about the book you are holding in your hands as I did about the one I was reacting to.

There's a remarkable scene in the classic *Frankenstein* film, where Karloff's creature gently hands a little girl a flower. This book is like that flower: a gift that reminds us of the humanity of monstrosity (as well as the universal monstrosity of humanity). Dietrich is a virtuoso of shape and structure, plumbing the profound depths of this metaphor. I can think of no other writer who bridges lyrical forms with genre material so artfully, wringing significance out of the neck of every word. *Universal Monsters* is an amazing accomplishment.

And so is *The Monstrance*.

Here we have a series of poems that harken back to classic monster movies all over again, with one exception: this is a *concentrated* study on one particular monster—the Frankenstein creature cobbled together as a trace memory of all the Frankenstein films and their derivatives from the period (and it takes liberties as much as it remains true to the series—I will not spoil the surprises by saying much more about this). Suffice it to say that this book is like *Universal Monsters* to the 2nd power, with a laser beam-tight focus on the biggest baddie of them all: the creature from *Frankenstein*.

Fans of the Frankenstein myth should leap for joy. Nowhere has the creature gotten such a seriously engaging and eye-opening treatment.

Dietrich has plucked another flower. He is handing it to you.

And yet *The Monstrance* is even more than this.

For this book is not just a study in monstrosity, or an ode to Frankenstein films. *It is an extended love poem, wearing the costume of horror poetry.* You get your hunchbacks and mad scientists, true, but it's the arc of lightning riding on the charged ions of Dietrich's depiction of the love between the titular creature and his gypsy dream woman that really drives this poem from beginning to end. You may not believe me based on the cover art or the title or even your perusal of the table of contents. But this book is a love poem. It explores all the facets of desire and communication and existential dread that any really good love poem should explore, but it does so by elaborating the conceit of a fictional relationship between imaginary characters torn from the expressionistic celluloid of yesteryear.

Why? Because that's what love really is: riddled with nostalgia, aching with fantasy, and messed up in monstrously messed up ways. And though the poem itself (and that's how you SHOULD read this book—as one big cinematically epic poem) is a bit of a throwback in its subject matter, it is a love story to that very past, and it is also therefore occupying a very present and contemporary subject position in relation to that past. And that's part of the appeal of this big, cinematically epic poem… it is a narrative that we can all identify with because we all have memories of the creature—even if they are just memories of our Halloween trick-or-treating—and Dietrich is a master at making us feel this creature inside of us in the here-and-now. If the creature (and all that he represents) is something that is undead and resurrected, that is only the beginning of something that Dietrich stirs inside of us, sparking to life our own memories of not merely fiction film but the movies of our own memories, the fictions we tell ourselves, and the desires we snuffed out and left for dead long ago.

The Monstrance, in other words, seeks to reawaken a passion inside us all that has been repressed. The poet embodies our own desire for reconnecting to the universal truths we've buried inside our hearts. It's uncanny how alive this creature—our dead pasts, our abandoned loves, our forgotten memories—really becomes in these pages. Whether it's a teenage love lost, a broken marriage, a broken home or simply our love affair with the movies of our youth, this love poem is damned good at making us feel something stir to life within us all over again. Sure, there's a lot of laughter and flight of fancy in these pages too—and I envy the newcomer to Bryan Dietrich, because there are a lot of happy surprises to come between these covers—but there is serious and sadness in this book, too. It's actually quite human that way.

And yet, once again, it is even more than this.

Earlier I suggested that the title of this book might mislead you a little bit, if you came to it thinking it would just be a book about a monster. It will also mislead you if you thought you were getting some theological text about the "monstrances" of the Catholic church—those crazy urn-like sculptures referred to in this books epigraph, that are intended to "demonstrate" the power of the body of Christ when they display the Eucharist. Yet this book does symbolize and embody a spectral power and that power is the language of poetry. If you strip away the conceit of the resurrected dead, what you have is something supernatural yet again: the word that makes things come to life. This is why this book works so well as poetry, and not simply as a gallery of character studies told in fictional form. This is as much a self-reflexive study of language as a "monstrance" of meaning as it is a tribute to old bolt-neck.

And yet, once again, it is even more than this.

Although the ambitions of this book are quite grandiose— for perhaps it is, after all, all about living "as best you can/between onslaughts of the divine"—one may still be tempted to read this book as a very personal, if not autobiographical, one since the narrative centers on the monster's thoughts and experience in a very intimate way, unveiling his desires and longings. You may wonder just what is this guy's obsession with gypsies and the undead, and who is this voice speaking in third person about all these things anyway? Who is speaking in this poem—and is he talking about himself or this imaginary character or *himself talking about* this imaginary character? Does he identify most with the role of master or creature or gypsy or James Whale or Mary Shelley or someone, something, altogether else? And the answer is simply, *yes*. Don't get hung up on subject positions. He is all of these things at once, a multifaceted voice centered in the wondering mind of the narrator—the poet giving voice to the words, the person who has absorbed and projected and mused over the meanings of these personalities that have been unearthed from his own imagination and experience. I think the poet would say the poem is about something much bigger than himself, but the personal feeling of this book is part of its winsome charm and you can't help but love what he's done for you by writing this book so intimately. Bryan himself in a blog entry once described his purpose as "trying to bring back…my ten-year-old sense of wonder, of paradox, of power" and in *The Monstrance* we can feel that very youthful sense of—and desire for a return to—these things. Poetry very well may be Bryan's way of holding on, of heralding, of making permanent through word; it also may be a process of unearthing and discovering new facets to the things we all take for granted. But maybe we also get a glimpse of that ten-year-old *wunderkind* growing up, becoming a bit older and wiser, yet cherishing and appreciating the past that grows farther away from us as we age all the more. For there is maturity and sophistication to the relationships depicted in these pages. In fact, it makes me maudlin to realize that the fictional relationship between the creature and the gypsy in this book is a lot more authentic than many romantic couples in the "real" world ever get to experience. If Bryan is a writer of the fantastic more than a romance author, the fact of the matter is that love is a fantasy, and Dietrich proves this the way all fantasy writers do: by taking the figurative and making it very real.

Though it is tempting, I really don't want to analyze any of the poems here too closely. I want them to speak to you in their own way, with Bryan's authentic, romantic, and fantastic voice. You'll feel the creature's power—and regret—and longing. It's there in the words. You'll feel like a pitiful thing when you walk as "an upright oaf" in his heavy wooden shoes, musing about the inevitable death that gravity always implies and identifying with the grotesque way our bodies struggle all our lives to fight against gravity's unfair weight. And you'll feel many more things that I dare not give away. Read this book in earnest—try reading it from cover to cover if you can—and enjoy the experience. You will learn that "The Monster's Last Lesson" is perhaps the greatest lesson of this book, but don't rush there. The ending will really get you, as all good love stories and horror poems and classic films always do. You'll no doubt return to it again and again. Regardless of whether you understand it all on the first read or the next, I know one thing. *The Monstrance* is a book you will not soon forget.

It will be with you on your wedding night.

Michael Arnzen
Pittsburgh, June 2012

*Have you never wanted to look beyond the clouds
and the stars, or to know what causes the trees to bud?
And what changes darkness into light?*

—Dr. Henry Frankenstein
Frankenstein, 1931

Frankenstein

Come. I'd like to ask you about fear,
about the nature of obsession.
Look, see that kid, scalpel in hand,
the bright, corpse and kite-crazed, pre-frocked teen
you thought you were before you woke up
here, in the middle of everything
you might have dreamed of? Is *he* really
you, and is *this* what you thought of, then,
when you rode those Gentuan roads
rain had claimed for river beds of tar?

Late summer, nights, driving back from some
town, when you crafted playful monsters
from each pale swell exploding along
horizons, from each touch of greatness
lightning teased from air, when each brief glimpse
down that black road only frightened you
more for the shadow that fell between
clarities, when you watched white birch bark,
limbs, flash in parceled-out rhythm past
the wagon—well, is what you have now
what *he* saw in those moments of light?

Or have you, as you pushed on toward
some home beyond the next slow rise, been
obsessed with blindness, with that long walk
in swaying timber where what you fear
is not behind you in a corner
of the fog, but there, ahead of you,
in a clearing like a tree aflame—
the directive of the ozone's arced
finger? Don't be frightened. Go ahead,
tell yourself this. Then live as best you can
between onslaughts of the divine.

THE MONSTER: Part I

I love dead...hate living.

—The Monster
Bride of Frankenstein, 1935

Bryan D. Dietrich

The Monster's Brain

Would the Master mind? He had a hunch
that sparks might fly, had half a mind
not to even *tell* the good Doctor,
figured, finally, it wouldn't matter
one whit. A few less ounces of pink
stuff, sure, but who's to say what's normal?
Besides, he didn't have the nerve.

The job should have been a no-brainer;
get in, pinch the merchandise, get out.
Nobody mentioned the damn things would be
so slick, he grumbled to himself, limping
back to the castle in a downpour
no amount of cursing seemed to stem.
Ghoul's night out. A little too familiar.

Hugging the bungled bell jar tighter
to his chest, considering its contents
sloshing about like chicken lo mein
heavy on the noodle, he wondered if—
having known things now from the outside
in—its woolgathering would loom less
carnal, its longing, less grave.

The Monster's First Lesson

"You haven't got a brain," he said, projecting,
it seemed, from that raw space beneath his hump.
Night of the fire. The Hunchback was teasing him again.
As always just beyond such playground as the chains
allowed, hard torch and easy insults at the ready.
"Just a lump of shit the Master topped off with bolts."

It wasn't as if the Monster could understand—
and neither was foolish enough to really think
so—but hatred, bud of the kind of love only
ancient siblings know, has little truck with language.
This was, mostly, *all* the Monster knew—this ragged
heap shaped like he must have thought *most* men were shaped.

So when the villagers came and the Master set them
free, when he found himself and that other forsaken,
there on the stone roof where even the balustrades
were giving in to flame, when the men below began
to call up for someone to throw the evil down,
he gave them what they called for, what they wanted.

The Monster Among Nightingales

I.

He sang, as best he could, among the leaves
whose lives he'd come to know as bed and board.
Atonal, guttering, broad and crude he soared,
nonetheless, on notes he'd borrowed, on sleeves
and coattails, on fragments which the waxwings
he'd found seemed, *themselves,* to clothe themselves in.
There, shivering and forked half-naked between
old limbs, singing as if to say mournings
never end, the Monster—confused, scared—
could find no way to name the silence friend.
The flames—though far away now, though long tiered
and tied to stone they still engulfed—had no end.
Wingless, a wanderer in the earth, disaster less
unreal than nightingales, he feared the fear of the masterless.

II.

Later, looking back, he'd mime to the Gypsy
how he thought the birds were screaming, afraid
of what flight they were capable of. How he—
lonely among those limbs, each yell a cascade
drawn backwards up his throat—poured bellows down
the surface of the bark below his perch,
unaffected, unaffecting over the brown,
matted moss, the nearby stands of birch
through which he'd run the night before, shivering
from a fire he'd help begin in hearts
of men he hadn't met—men whose siblings,
dead now, gone, might have been parts of his parts.
The castle in flames, the birds—to his ears—valiantly screaming,
he told her he sat there for days, being born, only dreaming.

The Monster and the Gypsy

No one, least of all the Monster himself,
expected he would fall for her. But night—
cast blue and green by the simpler magics
she knew so well—drew him into the circle
of her flame. She was a Gypsy, mostly,
motley and mysterious, cowled in a life
her hands had stitched together like her cloak.

And when he stumbled on her wagon, on her,
there in that thicket of poplars—so lithe
and smooth, dervishing in the dark—he could
not separate her body from the play
of light on wood. The cloak gave her away
though, and when, stiff, bandy-legged and frightened,
he came to stand before her—hands shaking,

stretched out, cupped, begging he thought for water,
for crusts, something from this warmth she half
controlled—she traced too carefully the life
lines of his wrists, his neck, the blue stitching
in his palms, cried. And, as he too let bright
water slip the ridges of each old wound
which bound him tight, she took him under her cloak

and into her wagon and played for him
a song that, like so many others, she
had piecemealed from the pine. He knew then,
here, in the shadow of a castle he had once
called his wife, his womb, how masters can be
chosen, how shadows take you in, how songs,
Gypsies, monsters, all, are cobbled from desire.

The Monster Nodding

Mostly, he could do no more than watch her
dream—this arch, that cheek, the instep of her back
turned toward him. And in the fire's timid
illumination, he would imagine
her naked, the moon's high sheen reflecting
from each small, elfish nipple as she moved
to a rhythm only she, the pale
chinaberries and the long mute know.

But often, when *he* dreamed of how he knew
she would hold him—close, wet, both a bit blue
in the weak light—he feared she thought he would break
apart, unpiece himself at the seams.
His Gypsy would draw back then, hesitant,
imagining just whose heart he had
inherited from his master's vast puzzling,
whose grasp, whose penchant for eggs and broccoli.

And would he—he could see her wondering—
would he want to chain her as he himself
had been chained, had come to know the language
of whip, board and bolt? Or would he count her
as he counted his beads, his poppy blossoms,
throwing the last away? Would he, innocent,
dumb, heave her into some strange body
of water, that womb from which he did not come?

Would he want to fork her with the lightning
he called friend, break her, stitch her into something
he could better recognize? The Monster,
waking then from these dreams, cold and frightened
in a night too near this burning, would watch
the firm rise of her chest and draw from her
body a surer, more seamless breath.

The Monster Learns About Fire, Again

Not *all* his scars were make-work of the Master.
It wasn't that he was stupid, the big lug,
and he didn't really *believe* he could pluck
and later press the petals of that flame,
but sometimes those with bigger chests—vast expanses
of bone to hide their hearts behind—harbor ships
there, not stones. Dream galleons, lost ghost schooners
whose maps deny the ocean has an end.

So when he grappled with himself afterward,
one hand lodged firm in a mouth too full of teeth,
when the Gypsy came and bandaged him, attempted
to teach him sense, how even the gorgeous
burns, he pushed her away, knowing already.
Those pained roses—now simmering, now fading
cold—seemed to pretty his joins with buds. Like bracelets.

The Monster and the Gypsy Join the Circus

I.
Daguerreotype

When the carnival came—all hurdy-gurdy
and conch music, all light and limb and breath
like caramel corn, pipe organ, October
bluster—when the wagons came spilling
over the hill near their camp, the Monster
saw them first. And seminal in that seeing
came color: motley and mahogany,
turquoise and teal, orchid, apricot, shades
of cerulean, of greened and reddish gold.
Banners too, flamed high in fragmented
tatters, portents of wind long gone in the tooth.
Stove in or whole, overrun with little
Turk boys, with the seed of several nations,
game and gimp, well and ill, the wagons caught
craw in his throat and there they seemed to stay,
hover, between heart and head, between one dim
luster—what they had—and another. The Gypsy,
alike enough to light on like dreams, took his
hand and together they approached that wild
din, looking for foremen, for home, for hire.

II.
Palimpsest

The circus, of course, adopted them. Wire
needed to be strung, holes dug, tent pegs filed….
And while the Monster attended to this,
his lover turned her hand at Tarot. Still, the tip she
got from a mark one day—months into this whim they
called their working tour of Europe, they
called their honeymoon—saying she ought

to wander down the midway, came, as revelations
go, as something of a shock. Her fiddle
in hand—the better, she thought, to field a truth
or two—she feigned minstrelsy till, undaunted,
she tracked him down at the sledgehammer booth. Bold
as you please, he was winning stuffed demons, Hades
hoppers, for some strange woman. He kissed her, loverly,
each time he rang the bell. Long after that seeing,
after the Monster had gone and come, had lost her
then regained what seemed to him the filling
for his life, his Gypsy pie, after they talked—over
whelks and warm vodka of storms, stars, his death—
after she'd long retired that violin of hers, she
would remember, still, how he had, only then,
seemed monstrous. How, there—among ligaments
of lumber, tendons of two by four, muscles
of many men, skin of scavenged canvas—
he seemed unsettling, a sum of sawdust
lost in sawdust, too appropriate for his
host, too much a circus himself, like
the ends of too many means, like the lost
love some clowns sew up in suits, like that
oafish fall so many think a circus will
redeem. And though she'd forgiven him by the second week—
had *mostly*—it was the first and last time she named him freak.

THE GYPSY LETTERS

*You think I'd wreck the work of a lifetime because
you're in love with a, a gypsy girl?*

—Dr. Gustav Niemann
House of Frankenstein, 1944

Bryan D. Dietrich

I. Constantinople

Okay, maybe we weren't *made* for each other.
You could be right. And he probably *is*
too tall, a touch tender at the edges.
But then you never wanted me to smother,
did you? Aren't *you* the one who always says
the bigger the man, the lower his hedges?
He doesn't try to keep me or make me
over, doesn't expect so much I want
to scream—you know how bad the others have been.
And really, Mother, he's no more ugly
than I am plain. See, *he* doesn't think that.
Unlike *some,* if you know what I mean.

Sometimes I imagine I can almost see
what *you* saw in raising me. The apricot
tree you helped me plant on the bank of the Seine,
the look you took from what I must have
trembled with…. I can catch myself catching *him,*
just the same. We built birdhouses together
last week. Yes, birdhouses! Would you believe
it? White pine castles to hang from trees, for when
we stop the wagon. And when we'd tethered
a few to our first ash, the most fetching laugh
chuckled out of him, and he smiled, and then,
Mother, then he wanted to dance. This Monster
whom I've never called a monster to his face,
this man who seems so awkward, graced with grace
of other men, this fellow with a love of lightning, lace,
graveyard picnics—he wed me to his long mismatched embrace.

II. Ingolstadt

The question isn't should I let him drive.
I don't mind him taking the reins, should
the occasion call for it. The question is,
how far to let him go. And it isn't even
the notion we would end up, barely alive,
half-axled off some precipice, lost in wood,
breathing hard, only mostly anxious.
No, Mother, my darkest suspicion
is I might like it. So why not give
way, lean back, loosen my little red hood,
forget the "appropriate" path, all else
that is, and let him paint my wagon?

It's so hard, though. To just let lust let go.
Hard to forget the me I had to fight
to get to this crossroads to start with. No,
I have a map. The map has lines, bright
divisions between here where I might
really be, here where I thought I should go,
and the X where the legend, in spite
of what I fear I feel for him, says throw
the beast overboard. I've beaten back
so many monsters before, escaped
across the edge of endless charts shaped
to the size of my resolve…. Now, still black,
blue, new lines appear between me and this man,
barely a man, between desire and destination.
I want to go, want to stay, want a plan to span
the span between headlong and hesitation.

III. Belgrade

You'd have thought I'd pulled the sky right out
from over him, Mother, the way he bolted
up, pointing, from my lap, to the horizon.
This was yesterday, in an open tomb,
picnicking as we waited for the rest
of the circus—all but the bears—outside Belgrade.
A storm was coming just over the crest
of some low hills. It was as if the Monster's god
had returned, come back for what life its son
had taken. Anyway, that's the way doom
seemed to have seized his jaw. The frightened pout
I've come to love (though deeper now) molded

that over-furrowed brow, and, nuzzling,
found my breast as I stood to stare down
the storm. The Monster kneeled against me,
the flat of his head—dark, damp hair—just under
my chin. I felt him sob as he drew me back
to the wagon. I thought he was afraid
the lightning would taunt him then take him home,
his mother unhinged at our dallying,
but when, at the first sound of approaching thunder,
he leapt from our bed and swept the curtains free
from the door, I watched him watch the stars unbraid
their patterns from a sky shuttlecocked to sack
cloth. Seeing his loss now, what he feared he'd miss,
I unpacked my scissors. I fixed it. We kissed.
We've paste paper stars now, on strapping strings.
Short sheeted skies hung from curtain rod rings.

IV. Florence

Did I tell you, Sis, how Monster almost left
once, how he thought I was an easy moon,
replaceable by fire? Okay, I know
how you loathe poetry, so I'll tell it slant:
It happened after the circus happened. *Theft*
would have been much easier, the heft
of such simpler loss, lighter. The blow
never hurts till it's stopped, till the slow
grind of bone is left to grow maroon,
the knitting skin ceded to a different loom.
It was a minor moment, I suppose—can't
you just *see* me pining away, me?—but rant

I did, a little raving too, when he came
home some months after we'd joined up, started
packing. He'd met his master's lover at the games,
won her a doll, become, once more, unhearted.
She too, I suppose. They'd been together
before—she, his first sight after the grave
exhumations, the stitches, the storms, bad weather.
Actually, he *did* go, for a time—saved
me the scene of throwing him out—but when
he came back less broken (though I'd ever
thought I wouldn't) I took him in again.

He'd grown some, beyond the old reins…. But, I've never
mentioned our freak show either. Its jarred child, glass-shod.
It'll never grow there—gone to whatever god
freaks go to—but in my dreams I set it free.
No running off to learn to run. It suckles me.

V. Göd

I've been channeling fairy tales on the way to Göd,
Mother. You know, Snow White, Rose Red, Rapunzel.
Even those no one knows—One Eye, Two
Eyes, Three. Ears of Wheat. Anything with Hans.
All tense innocence, all decidedly *other*, odd.
Girls seeking sex, axe, something perilous to nuzzle.
Womanhood, personhood, any good blue
blood to get carried away. A few even glance
toward true. Take that tale of the Old
Wizard. A young girl, unusual as usual,
headstrong—too like me, you'd say—wants
to visit the strange man who lives down the way.

Her folks say no. Too different. Too cold.
Of course she goes, wanting everything awful,
everything she shouldn't imagine. Haunts
are only haunted, she claims, when the living stay
away. First, she beholds a black man at his door,
then gray, then red, then, peeking in, finds a form
on fire, flames instead of head. Finally, he
lets her in, discerns her shivering, implores
her to share his stove, all she's seen. Warm
now, she begins. When, at long last, she
arrives at the final act, her catching someone,
some thing, on fire, he grins, whispers, *Come*
come darling, that was me, how I truly appear.
And I've been so very, very cold for so long, dear.
Then, waving his hands, he makes the bad girl wood.
I'm finding out, Mother, so much that burns burns good.

VI. Transylvania

Even a Gypsy whose heart is full,
who shares a prayer's delight, can learn to turn
wolf when the wolfsbane blooms.... The moon grows
pregnant tonight, Mother, and I'm remembering
Uncle, how they stormed the house that once, dragging
him to the river, how we dreamed him revenant, close,
returning some day for his Gypsy stick, his stein....
Is it always this way with our people?
When the torches smoke the street—the scythes' lull
echoing like soft water over cobbled,
stone cracks—feet meet feet to hobble
our love of night, to empty our eyes of the moon's full

cup, to drown us, stone us, fancify our ways
into ways of monsters. We are a motley
bunch, yes, a gaggle that breeds and spreads,
changes, like lyrics to old Bavarian
drinking songs, but we are not—as this pogrom
often claims—beastly. We are, at best, displays.
They see monsters in nothing but heads
too flat, skin too tan, say we nurture rot, we
influence, steal.... The clothes they make us wear
read more rococo every year, each new piece
a ragged graft to hide what hide they've added
to before. But I carry on. We've seen Nice
now, and Brussels. Wiesbaden was as near
to home as I've been in a while. I still get addled
at the strangest things though, Mother. Like how
much lover's skin you breathe in a year. Should it taste like snow?

VII. Venice

You've been dying to know, love, what it's like.
Well, Sis, dying doesn't do it justice.
Every night when Monster shambles in, comes
to me, stripped, his master's fine needlepoint stretched
tight, trembling to contain a love that's made him
large, I stare at him, hold him, clutch his length
of hair and claw him to me. It's my strength,
I think, the way I hold him down sometimes,
that keeps him satisfied. And me? I've touched
every whole of him, made love to thumb,
toe, that buckled knee, tongued his bolts once or twice.
I've even taken *him*, invaded, piked

him, cradled and stroked his cloven head
as he does mine—goading, guiding it free
from hood and shade, this wood of creeping vine.
Do you remember when we were girls
together, massaging trees to ease their knots,
conjuring mud pies—a *whole man* once,
remember?—from the clay of the occasional
crypt behind the occasional church
we were told to steer clear of? And how arch
those games began? How messy the miracle
of shaping became? And then the chance
brushing of breast on breast, the tease, the hot
growth of those tough, tube-riddled, bloody pearls
building in our chests. Do you remember when
game turned earnest and we tumbled finally
to earth? How we wrestled, always, with the dead?

THE LAME PRIEST'S EXEGESIS

*We must be more clever this time. We must pretend
to be friends with the monster.*

—Mayor of Vasaria
Frankenstein Meets the Wolfman 1943

On the Anastasis of Monsters

I've often heard a monster roams the heaths
around these towns, that he was thrown together
out of pieces from the ground. The wreaths

were not yet wilted when, untethered
from his time, he launched another journey through
this wood of Dante's, mine. I gather

he is guiltless for the seasons of his stew—
ingredients his maker must have dashed
in here and there. But what *would* Dante do

with such a soul, retreaded, dead, rehashed,
and what *about* those parts—the head, the hide,
a hanged man's heart, the lower left and slightly mashed

intestine of a Jew? A suicide,
a Muslim and a Christian and a slave,
a sinner, saint, pornographer, the pride

of Prussia's war—they gave their all to graves,
but now they give again. They pull, they push,
they grasp and grope and billow at the nave.

And when they die again, a sanguine hush
upon the lips, when Monster loses ghost
to phlox, to nodding onion slips, when lush,

false hellebore buddings bind his bones for host,
how will such attrition be regarded
down in hell? Which portion of which lost,

indebted soul will then return, re-sorted,
to save a former owner from his sin,

Bryan D. Dietrich

and where begin? Is one carotid

artery enough to shade the dim,
to add an accolade to he who's damned,
to teach a Stygian wader how to swim?

And what about that saint whose skull was scammed?
I can't imagine Augustine (or some soul
of his ilk) as headless through the grand

parade of centuries up there. His whole
would be diminished, and the Monster racked
up short, if part by part the angels doled

his better pieces out. Yet when their tack
has long returned all morsels, stiff or slack,
what then, when God's own Trump demands his borrowed
            portions back?

On My Library

At night, all my books rise up squalling
with the sounds of a thousand pages
tearing from the walls. The plunging Vs
of their covers—opening, closing,
flapping Donne and Darwin against the dark
clustering air for flight—lift them, swirling
like bad ideas of bats, madly,
viciously, and all the more dangerous
for the gilt on some of the pages.
But then, hovering like giant ghost
moths about my naked fixture, above
me, here in my bed, somehow still asleep,
they converge and descend and enter
me—the words, that scandalous ink, bleeding
back out like sweat into the blank sheets
I lie on. And when I am full, each eye
returned from its jog through favorite
passages, when I am packed up brimming
with the clarity of Calvin or the paled
ponderings of Pope, the shunned skin tones
of Sade, even the sea star shades of Verne,
when the shelves have grown silent and empty
and deathly dim, almost translucent,
I, too, grow faint in the absence and rise
and look about, and, finally, seeing
nothing out of place, vaguely hungry
but far too tired still to eat, I descend
again and fill the hollow I have
left with the question each figure makes.

On Absalom

'Tis said they eat each other.

—Shakespeare

Head to head they lie, simple, dead,
one composed, the other only
half so, like coffins rubbing skulls
in the grave. I came across them,
two crickets, outside my parish
on stone steps where the sexton
plies his trade with poison, and keeps
the population down. Last night

there were thousands of them, climbing
the smooth-faced sand, the blasted glass
standing between what they could not
know and what they must have perceived
as a kind of heaven. Mostly
blind, but for the urge toward each
other—*here* they found newer gods
under glass. Here, they put away

their progeny for hope, came to
lay siege to the call of the light,
that vision not nearly so clear
as even one pair of long, barbed
legs playing shadows into song.
And so much less immediate,
this light, so much more delicious
than the rough press of carapace

or the mandible's hinged caress.
These two—probably missed by chance,
by the mass exhaustion brooms know—
they did not dine at the same plate.

One, it seems, managed to find it—
eternity—in the sand, in that
single crumb of sleep strange sandals
left behind; the other, glory

in the hunger of his brother.

On Reasons for Going to Hell

I.

How about that first lie? Telling your mother
you lost the foreign offering, that it slipped
away like everything else. And remember
how she smiled, not understanding that she could
never buy your way into someone else's
mansion? Unless, on Sundays, you chose to rent.

II.

Or Fr. Tom's peep-box? The one with the sliding
door and the naked woman inside. Tuppence
a peep. Your first erection was a sideshow
at High Mass when you snuck in to free her torn
and tacky, sticky, paper breasts. He never knew
who took her, only you and your trembling hands.

III.

Maybe that time you thought Christ had come and gone?
Sitting on the porch, young, hungry and waiting
for your supper, for your father to return
from the fields. No one on the street, no one out
walking with walking sticks. Just you. You, knowing that
the man wasn't coming back, that you'd have to burn.

IV.

Definitely that day you came home to your
mother sitting at the table, crying. You
went to mix her some chamomile, and when she
said, "Honey, do you know what separation
is?" you turned to her, set her tea down, and all
you could think of to say was, "Oh. We'll miss you."

V.

It may sound silly, but there was that frog thing
too. All the other boys egging you on with
names like monkey-walk, mignon, prissy Christian,
names you hated. The way you hated the feel
of the toad in your hand. It was a stone wall,
good for dodge-ball. You dreamed that stain for weeks.

VI.

How about the child you never made, the one
you thought you could feel when that Thing camped outside
the parish one night? There are reasons you don't
talk about it. Most of them have to do with
God and waste. Not death, you never thought it was
that, but monstrousness. You felt it filling you.

VII.

Or the time you watched that body floating by?
It wasn't even blue yet, only buoyant.
Some girl had decided corpses come back
from voyages out to sea. An eddy, towing
her dark and draggled to the shore, moved slowly.
You didn't call the constable. Or close your eyes.

VIII.

So what do you call all this then? Is there no
redemption in interpretation, in crafting
metaphors from death, or suffering, or pain?
Your father called the landlord once, to complain
of sounds inside your walls. Some workmen came. They
sealed the holes. Those birds seemed to live forever.

On Conceptions

—for H. F.

I remember the summer when we were
pagans together. The time we rode past
a tent revival, him screaming, "Satan
lives!" just to get their goat. Oddly, it was

a full moon, then as well as now, and some
place in the time between, I found Jesus.
Strange how we wind up embracing corpses,
the ones we've tried so poorly to embalm.

And I'm driving home tonight, through this fog
that has risen up, unbidden, from red,
unfamiliar clay and yellow witchgrass,
watching it come alive like the fingers

of these withered trees it draws its shadows
from, watching streamers of darkness, of this
celebration for the birth of a man
he says was dumb to die, become pregnant,

shiver, and taper their umbilicals
back to earth in half-wrapped coils. Still, the night
seems to know the animals will never
really learn to speak. Though I believed it.

And I'm trying to understand. Is it
a love of antiquity, or simply
a crutch carved from rotting scrolls, from bones
no carpenter left behind? I've never

had much of a sex life. Is it worship
of the state I've sealed myself into? Hope?

A rationalization of the doomed
virgin I've become? Or, like Lazarus,
should I dream the hand to pluck me
from my narrow bed? He told me tonight
how his sister's child was deemed dead,
still walled in her womb, how they left it there

to grow black before robbing it at last
from that salt-heavy grave three days later.
He said they made her hold it, all shriveled,
bloody, silent in her arms before they

took it, cleaned it, and buried it again.
He watched me shudder at the thought, afraid
she might have needed that last clutch
at immortality, one final grasp

for the darkness that had been inside. I left
him with a promise to visit once more,
wondering how Christmas would find him next
year, if the fog would be as thick, if quite

so many would die again on this road,
alone, on the way home from where fathers—
like his, like mine—might or might not have been
waiting for them, us, patiently, all along.

On Darwin, On Wholes

We come in naked and go out dead.
Seems simple. Almost true. But really,
we're never the same people, no, not
even the same skin. And the organs
too—I hear the body replaces
those as well, cell by cell, every so
many years. Everything I guess, but
the brain—old minds on refurbished frames.

It should be a bigger mystery
than it is, should shake us to the core
to think we've traded off, by coffin
time, all that stuff we thought was us,
but then that's it, isn't it? Our thinking
doesn't change. These gray, alien sacks
of non-refundable ideas,
winding library corridors

seated so close to smells we almost
just recall, each arbitrary scheme,
fragile fretwork geared to keep us from
stumping our stupid toes, these brains built
on dreams' decay, on the several
shades of lost, burnt out races, prevent
our knowing what even stars must understand.
There's so much more behind us, so few

singular doors to memories we
can never comprehend, to smells we
barely even remember, and to
species we've known from the inside out—
so many holes, black or blind or worm
or no, to fall back into now,
that even this morning, slipping in
my shower, not watching what must have been

my skin slip down the drain, I only
saw the water, stuff I belched at birth,
only the slow rise of porcelain
toward a skull I have yet to get
to know. I couldn't see—at least not
then, when seeing *more* than me was all
that mattered—how we're never truly
naked and we're never less than dead.

On the Evolution of the Human Gait

So I guess like that of most upright oafs
my spine will be the death of me. These hacks
can't name it yet, but my osteopath,
my Science Age angel, calls it a secret
hate of walking right. Whatever. It feels

like skipping on stubs, like my ribs have struck
a bargain with my lungs. "Let's squeeze each
other free," they say. "Let the arms hang loose
from the brain for a while. Those devil hands,
they've been Judases for too many years now."

Not that I came here to bellyache—Lord
knows how I hate preaching. Still, it seems these
generations of walking a way
we weren't destined for have finally snagged us—
me at least—by the heels, maybe the crown.

And isn't the crown where most bleeding ends
up? Christ knows the thorny ones, real or not,
are hell on the disposition. But where was I?
Oh yes, this back pain. Sometimes I think
it's really history piling heaven

on rough columns of bone, that when we fall—
the past and I—gravity will laugh us
down, sniggering at the way we're always
reaching for grapes or God or some god's gun
powder. Aeon after aeon it always

comes back to bones, to rebellion. Luther
knew a bit about insurrection too,
about the body's rising up against
itself. And though his corpse couldn't admit

it now, he must have also known how all

we do, is done in passing, how you don't
appreciate power—the simple rush
of book reading for instance, or of asking
dangerous questions, or of prying this
foot-happy race from tar—till you've tried it

on your knuckles. Or here, flat on your back.

THE MASTER DIARIES

"Perhaps you will regard my work with ridicule or even distaste…. You have inherited the fortune of the Frankensteins, I trust you will not inherit their fate."

—Baron Wolf von Frankenstein,
reading from his father's diary
Son of Frankenstein, 1939

Jan. 21, 1870

Maybe the smell—cut grass, old moss, wet cobbles—
that, or seeing the Hunchback, healed, well, returned
to dredge the dungeon. Maybe his hunch, what I never
could ignore. Whatever it is, as the surrey
pulls from the castle—his mooned face in the tower
still waving—as I reach out the window to let
a breeze amputate the long, grey finger my smoke
has grown, something in that weakened wind reminds me
of the Crab Boy. That wasn't his name of course, just
what we used to call him. Church school, at recess.

We're all standing around the nativity, cold,
teasing the new kid—an ancient ritual, a jinx
of blood—but this time we feel the difference, something
tactile to taunt. He's poor, to be sure, but we don't know
enough, not yet anyway, to be against *that.*

Some say children beggar the angels, but when we
look him in the eye then, vagrant wind kicking loose
hair into our faces, and somebody says, "Go,
on, try some chin-ups, just don't cut Christ's roof in two,"
and someone else—maybe me, yes, I think, me—asks
him who he gets to shake his thing after he's pissed,
he cries a bit, raising two half hands to his eyes.
We turn away from this. It's not like we don't know—
we've seen him pinch at his food each day—we just
haven't mulled it over much, not really. All we do

is start the chant: *Doesn't have a way to pray.*
And now, still seeing the Hunchback, how his oval
silhouette recedes, his hand eternally raised, I realize
who I've hated since my monster left. And the wind?
It moves things, sure, but mostly wears them down.

April 13, 1870

I wondered when I set him free
if he'd escape the fire,
but in the melee that ensued,
between the burning, falling wire,

generator sparks, the ash
which frittered through the fray
like blasted, heat-blacked, lava glass—
the mirror shards that paled Pompeii—

between the cavalcade of stone,
the timber, tindered, cracked,
the rush of crushing, pitchforked men
who charged and cheered, ransacked

my father's dam's ancestral home,
between this, he...I...
there fell as well a curtained
caul, finale, a goodbye.

I have not seen the Monster now,
his lurching, halting ways,
for months that seem like blessed years
where hours blur to daze.

His footsteps have retreated, fled
this smoldering debris
where what I can't undo I did
to life's extremities.

The worst part is the *if* I cannot
abdicate, erase,
the if that does not recognize
the *then* I know is base.

I now believe I made him up
of parts of parts of scenes
of books I've read, or dreams I've had
of *almosts, likes* and *seems.*

Aug. 7, 1870

*I had thought I might send this latest muse to my friend the Parish Priest.
He doesn't get out much anymore—his leg and back kept him from seeing the
recent meteor shower. Maybe I'll just read it to him, our next tea.*

—H.F.

They come as fallen offspring of the sky's
mute womb, revealing in the sleeping trees'
horizons midnight's colloquy of lies.

As green takes on the weight of dusk, fireflies
strike spark, collect in clouds on mating sprees,
coming as fallen offspring of the skies

they did not form. This hub of dead men's spies,
solar center where fires freeze
horizons—midnight's colloquy of lies—

this is where they breed new hope, survivalize
the ritual of darkness that they seize.
They come as fallen offspring of the skies

that shadows know from shadow-like disguise,
but not from dawn's regret, or, yet, from these
horizons, midnight's colloquy of lies.

As lightning's children, none admit surprise
when showers shape a meteoric frieze.
They come as fallen offspring of the sky's
horizons; midnight's colloquy of lies.

Bryan D. Dietrich

Dec. 30, 1870

It's been a year, so help me, to the day
since I unleashed that Monster born of flame,
usurped my lord my God, forgot to pray,
and, as a body builder, came up lame.

What I unleashed, my monster, bore the flames
more readily than I, my fiancée.
I nearly bloody killed her with my lame
attempt at voiding her necessity,

her ready womb. I, my fiancée,
resumed our bland, doomed lives when he had passed,
attempting to avoid her old necessity,
that dream for children which our species has

presumed. We blanched then, doomed, living when he had passed
as if this race not born of lightning must
be dreams. And children? That which our species has
leveraged life with? I had made it just

a *simple* race, a boon of lightning. Must
she, then, have tried to join the circus to repay
that leveraged life I'd made? It just
seemed like *his* attempt to steal my clay.

She, when she left to join the circus—repay
herself—deserved better, a word, a goal. I pray
his seams will fail now, tempt time to repeal my clay.
It's been a year. *God.* Help me make another day.

Jan. 1, 1871

Does he contradict himself? Very well,
then, he contradicts himself. Take his heart.
Already it belongs to another. Eyes?
They, too, are drawn by a body peculiar
to his own. Blood, his blood, bends
to the beck of some stranger's caul.

Limbs, like empires, rise and fall, stretch
outward, always outward, toward territory
he doesn't yet suspect enough to want
to touch. Still, something, some feral power
frets him, forces him, forgives him
his awed, awful obsequiousness.

What is this fundamental fundament
of which he's made? What makes him—
crafted from everything other—want *another*
other, blueprint for all to which he's grown
so partial? Canals and columns, points
and pathways, lines and loops and aqueducts

and angles. Interiors, exteriors, the lot Lot
knew as maritime or manor, slips and ships
and steeling wax. He's made, he knows, of places
and spaces, steeples and peoples he can't recall:
Bachman and Brunner, Russ and Krause, Cowper,
Cooper, Darwin, Galen. Wharton's Jelly,

Sphincter of Oddi, Duct of Wolff, Anal
Crypts of Meera. What he holds inside what
isn't his isn't his. A body. And that body,
any body, is so much more singular than his own.
If only, he thinks, he could enter parts a little less
obscure. If only parts—his, others'—were half

of what he wanted, something he could take
to leave. If only he could part from this life,
this mad amalgam, so unctuous, odd, unfamiliar.
Each piece, a Bundle of His, a curse or, worse, gift
on his way to the Islets of Langerhans, the Space
of Disse, the Zonule of Zinn. What he wants

is anything *not* not anything not him.

Sept. 1, 1871

My priest friend and I have been discussing what books one should take to a
shipwreck on a desert isle, or Arctic waste...

—H.F.

The first should be heavy,
like a corpse, like foreskin
packed with riotous dreams.
It should make your brain hard
when erecting even
the most grotesque structures.

The second you should save
for Thursday afternoons
when the others in your
library have grown stale.
Read one sentence a week,
to keep what's absent holy.

If there *is* such a thing,
the third one, a fairy
tale, should be a touch more
bitter than the rest, should
remind you of crowds, crows,
disease, kingdoms left behind.

For variety, leave
the fourth to chance. Draw lots
from a list of your friends'
favorites. Or, to make
things more surprising yet,
borrow one from one you hate.

Number five can be fun.
It's okay. Your prison

will be dreary enough.
Unless the trees provide
the kind of pulp you'd need
for leaves to rewrite heaven.

The last should be slim, no
heavier than a flame,
should help you learn to lust
for sky again. Sanskrit
maybe, something ancient,
a field-guide to forbidden gods.

Oct. 7, 1871

So there's been some talk about the cutting
off of limbs, about the soul's reluctance
to amputate itself for the greater good,
but unless you've had an uncle with sky
where a hand should be, who scratched at that
blank space for years, at ghosts, the vestigial
kind, who know nothing of sleep, stumps or graves—
well, this past month won't mean much to you. Still,
seems everything, even my family
is falling apart these days. No, really.

I'm scared to even answer my letters now,
afraid it might be catching, might be caught
already—this, the latest in a long
series of strange dissolutions. My first
cousin? Both feet are gone, half a leg. My late
grandfather too—just one joint less to fret
over when the rains finally came. Aunt M.?
Doctor says her bones just dissolved. That foot
will never know her weight again, or falter.

And me—well, what with my queer blood problem,
the disconcerting way my arms go numb
when I've slept too long—I'm thinking about black
orchids, about gardeners splicing shaved
stems to breed a truer strain. And sometimes
when I find my head turning, lips half-formed
to ask her what to do, I remember
how I've lost *my* other too, those memories
outside myself kept safe in pageless books,
the ones she packed with half of what I once

called us—now, just me. When she left, I knew it
would be colder for a while, that the bed
would seem less hollow—more, from the weight she

did not think to leave behind. But I guess
October knows more about leaving than
any one man with two good legs, with hands
that still remember much—to shield the eyes
from wind, or chaff. Or smooth the sheets of those
who shared depressions, once, between weak springs.

THE MONSTER: Part II

*The lightning. It is good for you! Your father was
Frankenstein, but your mother was the lightning.*

—Ygor
Ghost of Frankenstein, 1942

The Monster and the Little Miss

No mother but the lightning, that which licked him into life.
No father but the tower with its crown of polished stone.
Who then to blame for the death of a little girl? Who
to finger as the framer of his ways? Master of his own
fate? Or collector of deceits, dissimulation? Who
formed his formless brain? There has been some talk about the rightness
of his rain, about the notion that his noggin needed
tending, that the Hunchback mucked him up with matter murkier
than the usual grey. His brain was pickled, they say.

But not kosher. So what about the Master? Or Lame Priest
who taught him penance? Who? Which Oedipus steps forward
as the founder and the forger of his crime? Men need mothers—
they, unlike the sun, shine always steady, true, sweating clean
the harsher burns—but fathers too? Is he *that* much like loss,
like oblivion, or do patterns grow from puzzles
put together long ago? Here, view him now, the Monster,
one leg up on mortality, one bolt shy of a barn.

He stands on the bank of the river, a daisy stem in hand,
its petals picked clean. He's been plucking them with a new friend,
a girl, with daisies in her hair. There is water, some lilies,
not a cloud in the sky. The water is deep, black, fast.
He is tall, dark, as handsome as the should-be-dead can be,
but not as fast, nor deep as any river, not here,
not now, not when the petals have run dry. There are pieces
he has never pieced together on his own. Questions
he will never come to answer. Death. Is it in him?

Does he know it like a song? Are the lyrics those of the Lame
Priest? Of the Gypsy? Of the Master as he labored
over roentgens, foot-pounds, ergs? Or, in this moment, glorying
in the sudden knowledge of this and like this, this and not
this, basking in that cranial flash of first associations,
with the Girl on his left, river on his right, stem
in his hand, petals petering out across a more
and more distant tug of water drawing them all to sea,

with something new on his mind and a lighter bounce
to his all-too-regular plod, in this moment when he steps
forward to trade ignorance for light, does the music he hears
turn on those fading cries, on the final suck of pigtails
waving the eddies down? Does he owe this choice to his body,
to the vast histories he's led? Or, in the sum of his parts,
in a heart he mostly calls his own, has he merely mislaid
some piece of mortal understanding? Has he always been
mistaken?

The Monster Considers Progeny

The Gypsy had stopped the wagon to shake her head,
to mourn the landscape France had placed before them.
Here, the Franco-Prussian war had been and gone,
had left its palette drying in the sun, and there...
and there...here, here, and again there, had left the tell-tale
signatures of masters: Doré, Goya, Bosch.
This had less to do with impressions than with bones
that cracked like blackened, once-green wood beneath their
wheels.
Not much is more immediate. So she didn't
take it in, but pushed the sights, the smells away. Monster,
though, seemed just as much at home as in a crypt.
For him, the niceties of burial were moot
at best. So when he climbed down and out, onto
that battle field, the plain truth of what remains
were left reminded him only of home. As he bent
to touch each fragment of what might have been
him, as he collected this moment, that thigh or rib
for future remembering, as he connected
these dry men with not his last thought of the young
Girl he'd tossed in the river, as he began
to recognize that there was such a thing as death
that didn't always deliver its components
back to solid state, as he considered
the options one has for faith in at least some sort
of continuity, as he reconsidered
the Gypsy, their love, these dead, hers, and all of his,
as he felt the unexpected rise below his belt
and grew—if only for a moment—ashamed
of all this death, he banished thoughts of little girls
to that sea where he knew at least one would end
up, and turned his mind back—as *he* turned back— to boats.

He had a thing for maps and ships, a bit of passion
for treasure, for the idea of it. He collected
them these days. *Pictures,* he could read. Wars, this one,
said *Hyer they bye monstyrs* at the edges, in blood.

The Monster Learns to Read

Byron, that pouting beast, he could take or leave.
Wordsworth? He could only pronounce him worried.
Too often the last part came out *warts*. And Keats, well,
who survives Keats? Now Coleridge on the other hand—
and though neither quite matched, he *did* have another—
Coleridge was chewy. At least as long as the poems
had demons, something *likely*, in them. Still, Shelley seemed
dead on—he had an eye for it, death, for knowing
what chains meant, and fairies, and fire. And the skylark,
so high, cold and far away—though he'd never seen
one—the skylark he knew he would know when he ate one,
slowly, sucking the soft parts clean from the spine.

The Monster Attends Mass

The glass people pictured there, pieced of fragment,
drew him that Candlemass to a low flame
not one of the windows *truly* contained—
rather, they only filtered the holy
light he found inside. There, in a filigree
of smoky amber, a priest's movements stained
the haze with dark trails of absence, laid claim
to each space his hands had been. Strange oddments
which the Monster could not name lay strewn about
the altar, called him further, past the door
and into rows of straight-backed pews the faithful
had abandoned as night drew down.

The Priest, lame but beloved by his town,
took the stranger who had come so late—papal
oddity that he was—in hand and lured
him to a small room where the Monster's doubt
was comforted by a hole in the thin,
curtained wall. Here, just short of speech, tongued only
with motions, able grunts, with the blunt, lonely
mainstays of the mute, the Monster named his sin.

Though they had found her, shaken, wet, a bit worse
for the river's wear, the Girl the town had thought
drowned, that reluctant flower the Monster taught
to swim, was safe now, sound. No lasting curse
would hang about his flattish head, no hail
Marys need be said, no rosaries counted,
no incense burned. The Monster rose, departed
his room, turned one last time at the altar rail
and balked at a stick there with a ball, a bell
at its end where it rested against the stones.
Inside it, the Priest said, were holy bones,
then laid it in his hand, a silver frail.

The Monster, The Master and the Windmill

So much like a sacrifice: Henry, the Monster,
caught up like wicks in a wicker man set aflame.
When the peasants came at last—angry, aghast
over the sheer audacity of his love for one of them,
the Gypsy's love for something they saw as less
than they (what for having once been more)—the Master,
one Henry Frankenstein, led the chase. And though they had to
swim, practically, through cardboard seas of carnival
oddities, castoffs, bearded women, little people,
those of the alligator persuasion, though even carneys
and barkers fought them for a while, the mob, the critical
mass of it, rousted Monster from his wagon, drove him
to strike his maker down, escape the circus and trade
his heart for the hills, little god in tow. Now, hand to hand,
embracing the more mortal side of combat, they seem to dance—
mad, inarticulate marionettes wed to flame. Here,
trapped between fire, fall, and windmill blade, unaware,
perhaps, of the Quixotic irony fate has found them in,
they struggle. One machine, one man. One maker, one
unmade. Shifting, changing leads, each step clocking them
closer to the sweep of the mill's strong right arm, one falls,
snags on a sail, catches it just long enough to understand
reach. The other, waking from ruin, will haul himself up
from ash, return to a ring not too unlike the one he'll give
the Gypsy, now that he is, as always, presumed dead.

The Monster's Retirement

He started, the Gypsy recalls, with scribbles.
Worked his way up to painting dead flowers,

roses taped to a wall upside down, each
petal grown crisp and cracked and black. She can

still see them, every purpled stem, like tintypes,
lifecasts cast from a green that sapped away.

And the frescos he painted them *on—God*,
hundreds of pounds. Layer after layer

of base coat, eggwhite, linseed oil, stuff
she made baklava with. Sometimes, she says,

it took months to lay a neutral surface,
a place he could finally, properly

re-inter the dead. His late period
dwelled on corpses, women for the most part

whose cold arms embraced nothing, whose slack breasts
lay sunken as only the breathless can sink.

Open mouths, open eyes, stale blood gathered
in odd hollows and straggling—a stiff

afterthought—in jagged twigs of hair.
This shift, she says, took years. From the bones

of flowers to voluptuousness. Blue nudes.

The Monster's Last Lesson

This is the word the Gypsy heard.

This is the Monster
who made the word the Gypsy heard.

This the Master
who made the Monster
who said the last word the Gypsy heard.

This is the madness
that made the Master
who built a monster
who'd say his last word to a Gypsy.

This is the dirge
that urges madness,
eggs on masters
who build their monsters
to say last words to Gypsies.

A sixteenth sunshine, eighty-fourth shade.
Nature's dirge.
The potion of madness
concocted by masters
who build each monster
believing in last words, in Gypsies.

This is the man a madman made,
a sixteenth sunshine, eighty-fourth shade,
the bar of a dirge,
a pinch of madness,
dash of Master,
every bit the dashing Monster,
one who'd say his final words to a mourning Gypsy.

This is the pie-bald crazy quilt,
the raggedy man a madman made,
sixteen in sunshine, eighty-four in shade,
the heat of the urge
where light found madness
and gave it the Master
to fill his monster
with fragments, words, at last to give the Gypsy.

This is the Monster the Master built,
pied and bald like a crazy quilt,
a raggedy man a madman made
from that six tenths sunshine found in shade
of funerals, dirges,
the hanging madness
that plagued this Master
and passed to his monster
and on to the words he'd finally leave the Gypsy.

These are the stakes one snakes from death,
betting on monsters the Master built,
pied and bald like the crazy quilt
wrapping this man the madman made
of a sixteenth sunshine, a bit more shade,
out of a dirge
and out of madness,
his own, the Master's.
And now the Monster
has learned a word at last to leave a melancholy Gypsy.

This is what journeymen build from breath,
snag from the stakes they've bluffed from death,
shape into monsters a Master built
of pie-bald patches of crazy quilt
that wrap this ragged, madman-made,
one sixteenth sunshine, eighty-fourth shade,
funeral-urged

piece of madness
of some Master
who's losing his monster
to a word. The one he's telling the Gypsy.

This is the death he knows to die,
learned from a journeyman trained in breath,
from pulling out stops from breaking death,
from being a monster the Master built
from a pie-bald life like a crazy quilt,
from being both ragged and madman-made
from that sixteenth sunshine, eighty-fourth shade,
from out of dirges,
and out of madness,
from the Master,
and now the Monster
knows what to say, a word to share with the Gypsy.

Here, on the bed where dead men lie,
dying a death he knows how to die,
lies a lone journeyman bartered from breath,
snagged off the scaffold, cheated of death.
Here lies the Monster the Master built,
a pie-bald, ribald, crazy quilt,
a raggedy man a madman made
in six days of sunshine, four eighths shade.
He urges a dirge,
free from the madness,
at last from his Master.
No more the Monster.
This is the word the Gypsy heard. Her first, his last, just *Gypsy*.

EPILOGUE

And now, once again, I bid my hideous progeny go forth and prosper.

—Mary Wollstonecraft Shelley

The Monster Returns

Later, after the brutal wake, after the organ
grinders and the bearded women, the tinier men
and the blockheads and geeks had left, after the barker
stopped attempting to charge for one last hideous glimpse,
after the chinaberries began dropping blossoms
on what simple stone grave the circus could afford there
beside the sea cliff, after the Gypsy—grown quiet
now, a certain sad glow adding mist to the motley
she wore—had eaten many a meal from the picnic
basket balanced lightly on his tombstone, after all
this, when that strange lump of a man came, bent and curdled,
into camp, a large bundle on his back, the Gypsy
never dreamed she'd find herself plotting resurrection.

Once she'd haggled down the price of the book—red leather,
iron hinges, pages burned clean of gilt—the Gypsy
carried it, that great plague of it, her Monster's Master's
diary, to her wagon. There, in the gloom of what
was left of paper lanterns, the pasteboard stars they'd strung
from the roof's ribcage, she began her education.
The three Rs: reanimation, resuscitation,
recombinant damnation. Tesla, Franklin, Galvin….
Learning at the knee of the master of all three, she
began to piece together understanding, enough
to scare herself, once again, into believing. This,
she thought, must have been what it was like for Frankenstein.
To smell God's sweat. To hear, in lightning, his knuckles crack.

Though she didn't have much money, no real hoard to speak
of, she began to collect what detritus was called
for—a Bunsen here, an odd lineament there, wrappings,
oils, lengths of copper coil, the occasional bell jar.
Some nights, she imagined herself swallowed up, indexed
by the damned book she'd plundered. E for eromancy.

F for fool. Yet when, at last, all she needed—the vial
upon vial of heavy metals, a good gurney—all
but the storm had been gathered, the rest was easy. Spade,
blade, unspooling the giant kite…. Such hubris, she thought
(as first one vast hand then the next twitched toward the light,
as she collapsed once more in the gravity of her
late love's grasp), such doomed delight, should, if nothing else,
keep

them both in stitches.

Afterword: Weird Sisters
Bryan D. Dietrich

I've been in trouble for loving too much ever since preschool. The first call my parents ever received about bad behavior came because I'd been catching little girls on the playground and kissing them. By first grade, I'd graduated to intimidation by technology. Several girls complained about the machine I created to make them fall in love with me. I had. They didn't. Second grade? My grandmother's back room, lights out, door closed, learning to kiss with cousins. Third grade? Robert Ford's lunchbox. It sported a peephole and a *Playboy* cutout inside. Lord only knows how many quarters I spent buying bliss.

Still, I don't know that it was the women *per se*, the girls, those strange and wonderfully different, slowly rising bodies. I suspect it was the love, my growing, gangly sense of it anyway. I remember surreptitiously watching 007's love scenes with breathless abandon, sneaking back to my room and tuning in on my JVC Videosphere, earplug in one hand, ON switch in the other, waiting to get caught. I remember tuning in to Hammer horror movies, drawn to the monsters, yes, but even more agog over each bared breast, each open mouthed kiss no fangs seemed to stop. In the epigraph to "Alastor: Or the Spirit of Solitude," Shelley quotes St. Augustine: "Not yet did I love, though I loved to love, seeking what I might love, loving to love." By fourth grade, this was me. I had fallen in love with love. But that same year I also fell in love with wonder.

It was 1976, the Bicentennial, two hundred years of history exploding around me in flag-print Formica, eagle ice-cube trays, Lady Liberty lounge furniture, Continental Congress cut-outs. Seems like that year was a year for more than just *American* mythology, though. It was also deep into the season of the witch, the season we'd begun to hallow horror. The 70s saw release of some of the greatest horror films of all time, the introduction of many of the genre's best directors: *The Wicker Man, The Exorcist, Don't Look Now, Texas Chainsaw Massacre, Jaws, The Stepford Wives, Carrie, The Little Girl Who Lived Down the Lane, The Omen, Suspiria, Eraserhead, Halloween, Invasion of the Body Snatchers, Alien, The Amityville Horror, The Brood, Dawn of the Dead, Phantasm, The Shining, Altered States....* Suddenly, Occult was cool.

Ads for *Time Life* books on the subject filled the airwaves, sandwiched between ads for the movies themselves, ads like, "It's only a movie, it's only a movie" and "Something beyond comprehension is happening to a little girl on this street." I watched them all during episodes of *Kolchak the Night Stalker,* during late night Hammer horror marathons, between double helpings of the Saturday *Creature Feature* where my father introduced me to the *original* horrors of Frankenstein, his son, his ghost, his house. Dracula. Wolf Man. Invisible Man. Wasp Woman. Cat People. Black Lagoon. King Kong (this latter returned that year to the big screen, back from the dead). Each one, a legend, each one a wonder. I couldn't get away from these lumbering, looming figures, from them or from what they represented.

My sisters started taking me to haunted houses that same year. My dad began buying me *Boris Karloff* and *Believe It or Not* comics, *Dr. Spektor, The Witching Hour, House of Secrets, Creepy, Eerie, Vampirella.* For my tenth birthday party, I asked to take some friends to a documentary: *The Mysterious Monsters.* The ad? "There are giant creatures living at the edge of our civilization." How could I resist? It tracked the biography of Bigfoot, the nesting place of Nessie, the hunted history of various versions of skunk ape and boggy beast from ancient times till now, and it purported to find at least one of them, the hairiest, still living in America.

Suddenly the monsters and their mythologies seemed closer, as close as the monsters on the covers of the paper packets I purchased from the ten-cent hallway dispensary. As close as the glow-in-the-dark Aurora monster model kits advertised in the backs of my comic books. As close as the books of mazes made in the shapes of classic monsters, as the monster stickers, the monster makers, monster tattoos, monster rings, monster cars. As *Famous Monsters of Filmland*. I remember Erich Von Daniken, his ancient astronauts taking the world by its reins. One of my teachers even used a film version, complete with singing crystal skulls, in science class. I remember the illustrated classics, *Frankenstein* in particular. And I remember, that year, reading the complete works of Edgar Allan Poe.

None of this, though, influenced me the way my sisters did, my own three Weird sisters, who read me horror stories from a book called *Strangely Enough*, who read me Le Guin and Lovecraft, Bradbury and Bram Stoker. Sisters who taught me about love, but who also taught me blood, bone, creature, fracture. As I've said, they took me to haunted houses, but not the placid peepshows we have today. These were hard core hauntings, back in the day when the players could still goose or grab you. I remember giant, encephalitic elves hacking some poor patient to pieces, harrying us through hallways of horror with a gore-slicked, severed limb, but I also remember my sister Cheri chasing me through the halls of our *own* house with a knife, acting insane, dragging her foot, moaning, "Hey nonny nonny."

They took me to houses full of haints, yes. They made make-shift haunted houses in Aunt Arleda's barn, yes (peeled grape eyes, pasta entrails). They read me stories, yes. But they also *told* stories, stories of the golden arm, of giant, marauding cats, of the pink ape and the chicken heart, of the thing at the foot of the bed. Once, my sister Heather dressed me up as the Hunchback of Notre Dame and took me trick or treating. That Halloween evening, standing on the step of some stranger's house, I playfully swung my swag bag at her and she flinched, lost her contact. I remember spending a good portion of that evening looking for her "eye" through my own fake, bloody "eye" as she explained what I'd been seeing lately, what was happening to our parents. You see, at ten, in the midst of all the horror, our parents were getting a divorce.

That Hallow's Eve I wondered, perhaps for the first time, *Is love a monster?* Looking for our eyes in the dark, dressed as outcasts, as indigents, we seek sustenance from those we don't know. We come to their houses, we beg indulgences, and in the glare of lights designed to show us for who we are, designed to let the ones on the other side of the door decide if they should let us in, blinded by blood and hunger, we lose sight of everything around us. It's not about what we choose to see. It's about what we *can* see.

The next Halloween, after the divorce, after I'd gone to live with my father, a local channel ran a marathon of Frankenstein films. Beverly and my other two sisters left their lovers at home, came over to watch the movies with me. We stayed up late, very late, long past the witching and into the wee, and I cried again and again each time the villagers misunderstood, each time others blanched at his reach, each time the monster got burned, buried, left behind.

During those early years, I remember seeing *Frankenstein: The True Story* (a failed fairy tale), I remember all the Hammer versions (failed, sordid sex), but I also remember other monsters left licking their wounds at my altar: Jack Palance as Dracula, a man who traded his soul for love; Vincent Price as Dr. Phibes, a man in search of his dear dead wife; Joseph Cotten as Baron Blood, a man cursed by a vindictive woman; and Herbert Lom as the Phantom, a man made ugly through the power of passion. Mad scientists, mad miscreants.... Like most of them, like Henry Frankenstein, I learned to populate my room with Bunsen burners and incandescent coils, ancient scrolls and singing skulls. Like Dr. Phibes, I learned to long for that love that might not return my gaze. Like Dracula and Blood, I felt cursed. Like the Phantom, I felt Ugly. Love and monsters.... Regardless of how I felt about girls, irrespective of how much I wanted a mate, I found myself as lonely as the monster himself, abandoned by his creator.

Through geek interests, geek eyes, I found out more about love than most of my friends, but *being* a geek made me a monster. The more I sought, the more they ran. And the more I learned to identify with Frankenstein's greatest failure. Maybe it's the creator myth that took me, maybe the notion of making the best out of loss (the dead), but more likely I loved this particular monster best because I also loved Jerry Lewis. As fate would have it, besides love and lightning, beyond battlement and beast, past the vast swamp and on to the things that matter, I also loved pratfalls. During the time I was learning how a home could become haunted, how monsters could mean melancholy, I also found myself watching every film Lewis ever made. I'm sure I didn't know it then, but my passion had drawn me to Shelley's demon's doppelganger. Jerry Lewis *was* the Frankenstein monster. Just as Dexter is today on TV, or Angel, or Monk, or Spock, or Sheldon, or Dr. Lightman, or Barney in "How I Met Your Mother." Nearly every character on *West Wing* or *Lost* or *Battlestar Galactica*. Oh, how we love our misanthropes.

It's not that I identified only with the goofball, the dork, the gangly, lost, and lovelorn monster. I did. I do. But I also think I identify with the creature's potential for eternal wonder. Unlike my preschool self, he isn't in love with love, not really. He's in love with how he loves wonder. Everything is possible for him. Every possible possibility is multiplied for him—how many other wonderers is he made of? He wanders the swamp looking for meaning. He asks his maker for another like him. He braves storm and sea, frozen families and frozen tundra to find that connection which might just spark, once more, the sublime that gave him life.

Like the monster, I have chosen seeking itself as my profession. Like the monster, I have found it both rewarding and revelatory. But, like the monster, I have also found that, without the proper perspective provided by a mate, the seeker becomes buffoon. In recent years, marrying for a third and final time, I managed to find the *right* mate, a woman whose interests are my own, who can quote *The Shining* and *Young Frankenstein* as easily as Shakespeare, who does not find my observation about her recent operation troubling (turns out that neck fusion involves inserting bone material from the dead, as well as neck bolts). The fact that she was once electrocuted is only added symbolic bonus. Still, this is not the norm. I know that the ten-year-old me felt as lost as that creature wandering the outskirts of Ingolstadt, raising his hands toward music he barely understood, and I know that the me, now, cries every time that image emerges from the past like a black and white film watched on a black and white TV under a black and white blanket with my sisters who held me and told me, *Wait, just wait, be patient.* Your living dead girl is out there, somewhere.

So, here is this book. Once upon a time, it spoke to the love I found with Alice, the woman who would become my second wife. Once upon a time, a version of it became my dissertation. Today, I think it still speaks to what I love, what I wonder over, what I've made a life from. It gathers the pieces of all that still seems terribly important. I hope it speaks to that which drives us all to rise, rise and walk. If a funny man can be Frankenstein's familiar, then what is the distance, really, from love to wonder? What might we find on Mont Blanc, in the blank space of that unending, ineffable, arctic wasteland? What do we chase but that which made us?

One final observation. One I left out earlier. One last piece before I end with another last piece (there's always one more in the graveyard). One last exhumation before I let you go to sleep with the tale of "The Golden Arm" creeping into your dreams, the sound of sisters telling ghost stories by flashlight...In the seventies, Topps created a series of trading cards called "You'll Die Laughing." Each featured creatures from the Universal monsters era. Each boasted the image of a classic monster and a joke. Many sported similar tableaus: giant robot with a woman in his arms, werewolf with a woman in his arms, mummy with a woman in his arms. Saucer man, ape man, man-like creature from black lagoon, man made of corpses. All with women in their arms. I collected every one. Those cards came as prizes in a particular brand of bread, the staple, the staff of life called Wonder.

CREATURE COMFORTS

Dead Man, Doomsday, Dr. Doom,
see-through creature from Black Lagoon.
A headshot, signed, of Captain Sulu.
Betentacled, bloodshot, plush Cthulhu
propped against a lunch pail lid
detailed in *Night of the Living Dead.*

Assorted skulls of painted plaster:
Maori nightmare, cask disaster.
A knock-off danse macabre relief—
butcher lecher, skeleton thief—
corner cobweb, bottom row,
erected by the collected Poe.

From chemistry failure, acid bottles.
Black plastic scorpions, Tlazolteotl's
child-chocked lap, her teeth hard set,
image of Senenahemthet.
Horus-Aah, the Chinese Immortals,
Buddha of boredom, Buddha of chortles.

Here, an acupuncture doll,
his regions quartered, skeined, in thrall
to numbered veins of blue and black
and points for planning pin attack.
A Dalek. A ring too like Hal Jordan's.
Leatherface, Jason, Lizzie Borden's

exsanguined cheeks, her simulacrum.
A gargoyle to guard this godforsaken
land of books, this trackless bracken.
One head, neckbolts, another, shrunken.
An Austrian wedding clock, still broken.
A backstage pass to hell, small token.

Frazetta's rosettas of well-drawn bras,
cups spilling over, crystal balls.
A fossil fish, 7,000,000 year ichth.
Vampirella with stake, barely a stitch.
Pewter dragon, Vader bust,
a batwinged, resin succubus.

Other lusts, my wife, divine,
an eagle from *Space 1999*.
Die-cast vessels, a few lost wax,
a Martian saucer from *Mars Attacks*.
A faux Sojourner, the Enterprise,
gumball aliens with green apple eyes.

Dr. Zeus, Nosferatu,
Gort the robot, sans his Klaatu,
the Phantom of the Paradise,
and here behind my ether eye's
own omnium gatherum, cathode stare,
a final poster: THE TRUTH'S OUT THERE.

My office, my space, my bag of tricks,
my books, my life, my itch for kitsch....
It's what I've wanted since I was green,
this lust for Aurora's Monster Scene
Custom Builder Mad Lab Kit,
complete with victim, dungeon pit.

I saw the ads in pulps like *Strange*,
knew when I grew to rearrange
a room of my own without cute cats,
no clowns or bunnies but Willard's rats,
I'd stock the shelves with spines, with books
then flesh the rest with the weird in nooks.

I'd gather together dread dioramas,

people my steeple with gothic dramas:
Dracula fresh from coffin seat,
mad doctor, mad doctor, the Mummy complete
with miniature canopic jars….
I know St. Vitus, just hum a few bars.

So monsters dance between my pages,
hobgoblins hobnobbing poets, sages,
and somewhere, boxed under basement stairs,
a horror comic still prepares
that ten-year-old to draw, devour
poetry from *The Witching Hour.*

About the Poet

Bryan D. Dietrich is the author of six books of poems and a book-length study on comics. He is also co-editor of *Drawn to Marvel*, an anthology of superhero poetry.

His poetry has been published in *The New Yorker*, *The Nation*, *Poetry*, *Ploughshares*, *Weird Tales*, *Asimov's*, *Harvard Review*, *Yale Review*, and many other journals. Bryan has won numerous awards for his work, including the *Paris Review* Prize and an *Asimov's* Readers' Choice Award, and has been nominated for both the Pushcart and the Pulitzer.

Professor of English at Newman University, Bryan lives in Wichita, Kansas with his wife, Gina, their son, Nick, and three cats...one of them evil.

Visit his website at: http://www.bryandietrich.com/

Printed in the USA
CPSIA information can be obtained
at www.ICGtesting.com
LVHW020248230724
786246LV00001B/111